ZONDERVAN

Praying Circles Around Your Future
Copyright © 2018 by Mark Batterson

This title is also available as a Zondervan ebook.

Requests for information should be addressed to:
Zondervan, 3900 Sparks Dr. SE, Grand Rapids, Michigan 49546

ISBN 978-0-310-76615-5

Author is represented by the literary agency of
The Fedd Agency, Inc., P.O. Box 341973, Austin, Texas, 78734

Interior design: Rob Monacelli / RAM Creative

Printed in China

18 19 20 21 22 /DCI/ 22 21 20 19 18 17 16 15 14 13 12 11 10 9 8 7 6 5 4 3 2 1

Praying Circles

Around Your

Future

New York Times bestselling author

Mark Batterson

Don't let what you cannot do keep you from doing what you can.

Draw the circle.

Don't let who you aren't keep you from being who you are.

You're a circle maker.

Israel's history is full of tough spots, but the first century BC was one of the worst. An entire generation was on the brink of death because of a drought. And worse, God was nowhere to be heard. But there was one man who dared to pray anyway: Honi.

That day was the day the legend of the circle maker was born.

With a six-foot staff in his hand, Honi began to turn like a math compass as the crowd looked on. In the center of the circle he had shaped with his staff, Honi dropped to his knees and raised his hands to heaven. With authority like the prophet Elijah's, Honi called down rain: "Lord of the universe, I swear before Your great name that I will not leave this circle until You have mercy upon your children."

As his prayer ascended to the heavens, raindrops descended to the earth. All eyes looked to the sky, but Honi's head remained bowed. Still kneeling within the circle, Honi lifted his voice over the sounds of celebration: "Not for such rain have I prayed, but for rain that will fill cisterns, pits, and caverns."

The sprinkle turned into such a torrential downpour that the heavens roared. It rained so heavily and so steadily that the people fled to the Temple Mount to escape flash floods. Honi stayed and prayed in his fading circle. Once more he refined his bold request: "Not for such rain have I prayed, but for rain of Your favor, blessing, and graciousness."

Then the perfect rain shower began to calmly cover the dead and thirsty ground, filling the air with a gentle, peaceful mist. Every raindrop was a sign of God's grace, soaking the spirit and refreshing the faith of all who were there that day. It was difficult to believe before that day. After that day, it was impossible not to believe.

The prayer that saved a generation was deemed one of the most significant prayers in Israel's history, and the legend of the circle maker stands forever as a testament to the power of a single prayer to change the course of history.

God isn't offended by your

BIGGEST DREAMS

or your

BOLDEST PRAYERS.

He's offended by

anything less.

BOLD PRAYERS

HONOR GOD *and* GOD HONORS BOLD PRAYER

There is nothing GOD loves
more than keeping promises,
answering prayers,
performing miracles,
and fulfilling dreams.

That is *who* He is.
That is *what* He does.

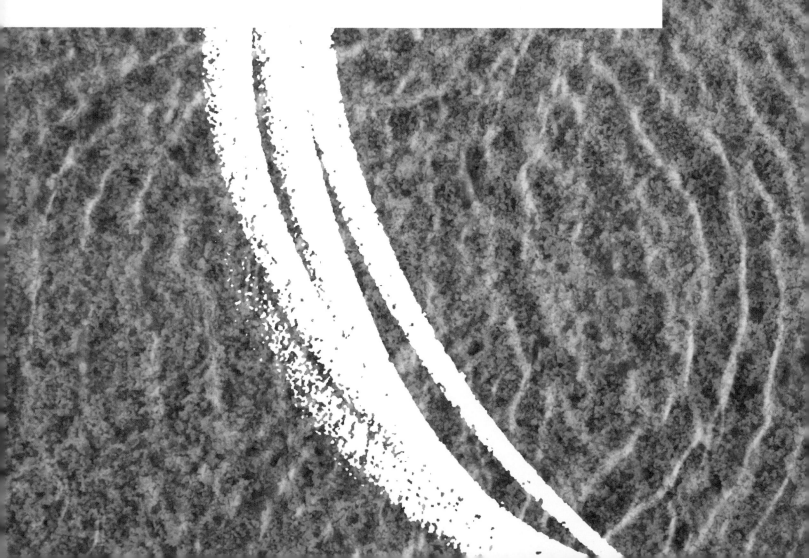

The greatest moments in life are the miraculous moments when human weakness and divine power intersect

and they intersect when we draw a circle
around the impossible situations in our lives
and invite God to intervene.

Prayer is the
difference
between the
best you can
do and the best
God can do.

GOD HAS YOU

RIGHT WHERE HE WANTS YOU.

WHO YOU BECOME

is determined by

HOW YOU PRAY.

You aren't called to live in the shadow of doubt. Instead, you can live with a holy anticipation because you never know how or when or where

GOD IS GOING TO ANSWER YOUR PRAYERS.

God has the ability to answer the prayers we should have prayed but lacked the knowledge or ability to even ask.

The greatest tragedy
in life is the prayers
that go unanswered
because they go

UNASKED.

What promise are you
praying around?

What miracle are you
marching around?

What dream does your
life revolve around?

Just like Honi,
YOUR PRAYERS
HAVE THE POTENTIAL *to change the* COURSE OF HISTORY.

In the grand scheme of God's story,
there is a footnote behind every headline.

The footnote is

PRAYER.

And if you focus on the footnotes,
God will write the headlines.
It's your prayers that change the eternal plotline.

You are always only one
prayer away from a miracle.

NTERCEDE

UNTIL GOD INTERVENES.

If you want God to do something new in your life, you can't do the same old thing.

YOU'VE GOT TO DO SOMETHING DIFFERENT.

It will involve more sacrifice, but you'll get to a place where you're so close to God that you will realize that you sacrificed very little in comparison to what you receive.

There will always be higher heights
and deeper depths in prayer,
and God wants to take you there.

He wants to take you to places
you have never been before.

Prayer and imagination are directly proportional: the more you pray the bigger your imagination becomes because the Holy Spirit supersizes it with God-sized dreams.

Nothing honors God more than a big dream that is way beyond our ability to accomplish.

Why?

BECAUSE THERE'S NO WAY WE CAN TAKE CREDIT FOR IT.

And nothing is better for our spiritual development than a big dream because it keeps us on our knees in raw dependence on God.

DREAMING REALLY IS A FORM OF PRAYING,

AND PRAYING IS A FORM OF DREAMING.

Once you embrace
the unlimited power
of God, you'll draw
bigger and bigger circles
around your God-given,
God-sized dreams.

If you've never had a God-sized dream
that scared you half to death,
then you haven't really come to life.

If you've never been overwhelmed by
the impossibility of your plans,
then your God is too small.

If your vision isn't perplexing and impossible,
then you need to widen the diameter
of your prayer circles.

By definition, *a big dream is a dream that is bigger than you.* In other words, it's beyond your ability to accomplish. And this means there'll be moments when you doubt yourself. But that's when you need to remind yourself that your dream isn't bigger than God.

FACING YOUR FEARS

is the beginning of the battle.

Circling them over and over again
is the rest of the story.

With God, it's never an issue of
"CAN HE?"

It's only a question of
"WILL HE?"

And while you don't always know *if* He *will*, you should always know that He *can*.

And because you know He can, you can pray with holy confidence.

The size of our prayers depends on the size of our God.

And if God knows no limits, then neither should our prayers.

With God, there is

NO BIG OR SMALL, EASY OR DIFFICULT, POSSIBLE OR IMPOSSIBLE.

IS YOUR DREAM
TOO BIG FOR YOU?

It better be, because that will force you to pray circles around it. If you keep circling it in prayer, God will get bigger and bigger until you see your impossible prayer for what it really is: an easy answer for an almighty God.

True faith doesn't just celebrate after the miracle has already happened; true faith celebrates before the miracle happens, as if the miracle has already happened, because you know that God is going to deliver on His promise.

Even if God doesn't answer the way you want,

YOU STILL NEED TO PRAISE THROUGH.

That's when it's most difficult to praise God, but that is also when our praise is most pure and most pleasing to God.

There is no **EXPIRATION DATE** on prayer.

OUR PRAYERS don't die when we do.

They live on long **AFTER WE'RE LONG GONE.**

GOD LOVES SHOWING UP

IN UNEXPECTED WAYS AT UNEXPECTED TIMES.

He allows our small plans to fail so that
His big dream for us can prevail.

No doesn't always mean no;
sometimes no means not yet.

We're too quick to give up on God when
He doesn't answer our prayers when we
want or how we want.

Never put a comma
WHERE GOD PUTS A PERIOD,
and never put a period
WHERE GOD PUTS A COMMA.

Is there some dream that God wants to resurrect?

Is there some promise you need to reclaim?

Is there some miracle you need to start believing for again?

The only way you can fail is if you

STOP PRAYING.

THE DEATH OF A DREAM

is often a subtle form of idolatry.

We lose faith in the God who gave us the big dream and settle for a small dream that we can accomplish without His help.
We go after dreams that don't require divine intervention.

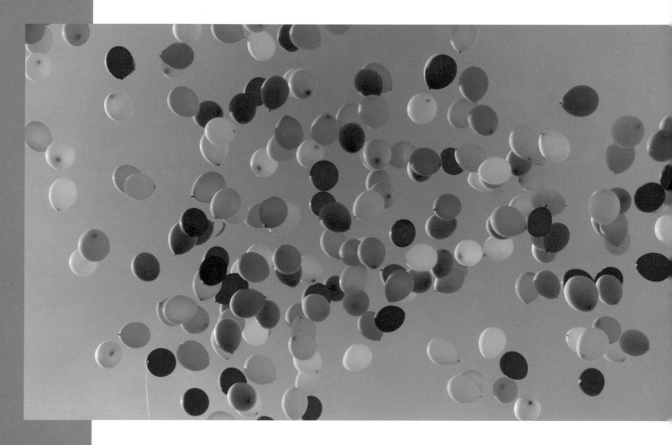

If you want God to surprise you, you have to give up control. You will lose a measure of predictability, but you'll begin to see God move in uncontrollable ways!

God is infinitely

BIGGER

THAN YOUR BIGGEST PROBLEM

or

BIGGEST DREAM.

Never underestimate
the power of a single
prayer. God can do
anything through
anyone who circles
their big dreams
with bold prayers.

With God, there
is no precedent,
because all things
are possible.

ONE BOLD PRAYER

can accomplish more than a
thousand well-laid plans.

God doesn't do miracles to satisfy our selfish whims. God does miracles for one reason and one reason alone:

TO SPELL HIS GLORY.

We just happen to be the beneficiaries.

Drawing prayer circles around our dreams isn't just a mechanism for accomplishing great things for God; it's a mechanism God uses to accomplish great things in us.

CIRCLE MAKERS
are RISK TAKERS.

IF YOU DON'T TAKE
THE RISK,

YOU FORFEIT
THE MIRACLE.

Drawing prayer circles often looks like an exercise in foolishness.

BUT THAT'S FAITH.

Faith is the willingness to look foolish.

Sometimes faith seems like a denial of reality, but that's because we're holding on to a reality that is more real than the reality we can perceive with our five senses.

It often seems like circling the promises of God is risky, but it's not nearly as risky as *not* circling the promises of God. The greatest risk is failing to circle the promises of God because we forfeit the miracles God wants to perform.

LOGIC
IS SCREAMING NO;

FAITH
IS WHISPERING YES.

Too often we let how get in the way of
what God wants us to do. We can't figure out
how to do what God has called us to do,
so we don't do it at all.

If you put what little you have in your hand into the hand of God, it won't just add up;

God will make it multiply.

YOU'LL NEVER OUT-GIVE GOD.

It's not possible, because God has promised that in the grand scheme of eternity He will always give back more than you gave up.

If you aren't willing to
put yourself in

"THIS IS CRAZY"

situations,
you'll never experience

"THIS IS AWESOME"

moments.

GOD DOESN'T CALL THE QUALIFIED;
GOD QUALIFIES THE CALLED.

IF YOU PRAY THROUGH,
GOD WILL COME THROUGH.

Sometimes the power of prayer is the power to

CARRY ON.

It doesn't always change your circumstances, but it gives you the strength to walk through them. When you pray through, the burden is taken off of your shoulders and carried by your Savior, who carried the cross to Calvary.

We sometimes pray like God doesn't *want* to keep His promises, and we have to beg Him to. You have no idea how badly

GOD WANTS TO KEEP HIS PROMISES!

That's why He made them in the first place.

God isn't holding out or holding
back at all. It's not in His nature to
withhold any good thing from us.

If you take God at His word, it takes a load off your shoulders, because you realize He wants to

BLESS YOU

far more than you even want to be blessed. And His capacity to give is far greater than your capacity to receive.

PRAYING HARD

is standing on the promises of God.

And when we stand on His word,
God stands by His word.
His word is His bond.

There is nothing God loves more than keeping His promises. He is actively watching and waiting for us to simply take Him at His word. He's watching over each and every promise that He's made, and if that doesn't fill you with holy confidence, what will?

Long before you woke up this morning and long after you go to sleep tonight, the Spirit of God was circling you with songs of deliverance.

He has been circling you since the day you were conceived, and He'll circle you until the day you die. The Holy Spirit is praying hard for you with groans that can't even be translated into human language.

Praying hard is trusting that God will fight our battles for us. It's the way we take our hands off the challenges we face and put them into the hands of God Almighty.

And He can handle them.

The hard thing about praying hard is

LETTING GOD DO THE HEAVY LIFTING.

You have to trust the favor of God to do for you what you cannot do for yourself.

We want things to happen at the speed of light instead of the speed of a seed planted in the ground.

We want our dreams to become reality overnight.

We want our prayers answered immediately, if not sooner.

But the key to dreaming big and praying hard is

THINKING LONG.

We want to reap the second after we sow, but this isn't the way it works with

DREAMING
BIG *and*
PRAYING HARD.

Each prayer is like a seed that gets planted in the ground. It disappears for a season, but it eventually bears fruit that blesses future generations. In fact, our prayers bear fruit forever. Prayer is a timeless seed.

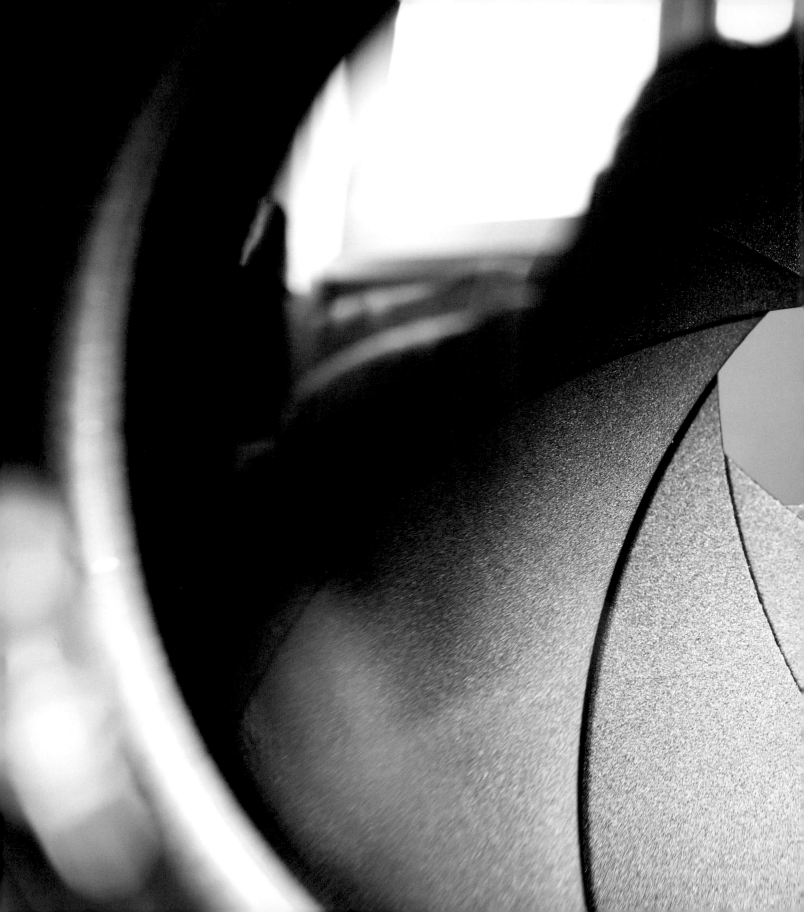

Prayer doesn't just change circumstances; more important, it changes *us*. It doesn't just alter external realities; it alters internal realities so that we see out of a different lens.

PRAYING THROUGH

can be long and boring, but it's the

Just as our greatest successes often come on the heels of our greatest failures, our greatest answers to prayer often come on the tail end of our longest and most boring prayers.

It's not just where
you end up that's
important;
it's how you get there.
THE HARDER THE BETTER.
It's true in life; it's true in prayer.

PRAYER IS PRIMING.

Prayer puts us in a spiritual frame of mind. Prayer helps us see and seize the God-ordained opportunities that are all around us all the time.

When was the last time you found yourself flat on your face in prayer?

When was the last time you got sore knees kneeling before the Lord?

When was the last time you pulled an all-nighter in prayer?

Prayer is the difference between

LETTING THINGS HAPPEN
and
MAKING THINGS HAPPEN.

What seems like an unanswered
prayer means that

GOD HAS A BETTER ANSWER.

Do you trust that God is for you even when He doesn't give you what you asked for? Do you trust that He has reasons beyond your reason? Do you trust that His plan is better than yours?

Our heavenly Father is far too wise and loves us far too much to give us everything we ask for. Someday we'll thank God for the prayers He didn't answer as much as or more than the ones He did. Our frustration will turn to celebration if we patiently and persistently pray through.

SOMETIMES GOD
gets in the way to
SHOW US
THE WAY.

Divine detours
often get us
where God
wants us to go.

BETTER DOORS.

If you want to see

CRAZY MIRACLES,

obey the crazy promptings
of the Holy Spirit.

The more opposition we experience,
the harder we have to pray,

and the harder we have to pray,
the more miracles God does.

Maybe you're in a desperate situation right now. That means one thing:

GOD IS SETTING THE STAGE FOR A MIRACLE.

GOD
ALWAYS RECYCLES
OUR MISTAKES.

God is great not just because
nothing is too big for Him;
God is great because nothing is
too small for Him.

If you want to experience a supernatural breakthrough, you have to pray through. But as you get closer to the breakthrough, it often feels like you're about to lose control, about to fall apart. That's when you need to press in and pray through.

What if we converted every problem, every opportunity, into a prayer? What if we stopped reading the news and started praying it? What if lunch with friends turned into prayer for your friends? Maybe we'd come a lot closer to our goal: praying without ceasing.

You can't just be willing to **PRAY ABOUT SOMETHING;** you also have to be willing to do a thing or two about it.

Never underestimate the **POTENTIAL** *of* **ONE RESOLUTION** *to change* **YOUR LIFE.**

The best prayer doesn't even involve words at all; the best prayer is a life well lived. All of life is meant to be a prayer, just as all of life is meant to be an act of worship.